AMERICAN
INMATE

AMERICAN
INMATE

Justin Rovillos Monson

Haymarket Books
Chicago, Illinois

Published in 2024 by
Haymarket Books
P.O. Box 180165
Chicago, IL 60618
773-583-7884
www.haymarketbooks.org
info@haymarketbooks.org

ISBN: 978-1-64259-973-2

Distributed to the trade in the US through Consortium Book Sales and Distri-
bution (www.cbsd.com) and internationally through Ingram Publisher Services
International (www.ingramcontent.com).

This book was published with the generous support of Lannan Foundation,
Wallace Action Fund, and Marguerite Casey Foundation.

Special discounts are available for bulk purchases by organizations and institu-
tions. Please email info@haymarketbooks.org for more information.

Cover artwork, *Aaron*, from "Composite of Knowledge" © Samuel Rodriguez,
published with permission from the artist.

Printed in Canada by union labor.

Library of Congress Cataloging-in-Publication data is available.

10 9 8 7 6 5 4 3 2 1

Attention: Any likeness of stories or characters to real events or people in this
book is entirely coincidental and/or a work of creative poetic documentation.

This isn't for the shook ones.
It's for my dogs in lockup, who have lived these
words with me.
For my family, who has held me down and kept me
up to the fullest.
For J, who walks with me.

: *America. God bless you if it's good to ya.*
America, please take my hand,
can you help me underst—[*]

: *If I'm transformed by language, I am often*
crouched in footnote or blazing in title.
Where in the body do I begin?[†]

[*] Kendrick Lamar, "XXX."
[†] Layli Long Soldier, *Whereas*

TRACK LIST

IV.

: I don't know how to start this shit.[*]

: Let those I love try to forgive what I have made.[†]

[*] Nas, "N.Y. State of Mind"

[†] Ezra Pound, *Cantos*

INTRO

featuring JAY-Z

I don't know how I ended
up here. Yeah, actually I
know. I called it.   I made myself

a dumb prophet & cuffed my own
wrists like a God who creates
& creates   & creates   too

many worlds to wave his hand   or
whatever he believes he's doing
              over & grant the prayers

of his reckless children. He gets
mad because he gets shown up.   He
fails at the feet of his

creations. I know how
I got here. When I first came
down they measured my criminal

mindset by sitting me down
in a small room   an office
          giving me a battery

of statements: *If my family*
gets hurt then I feel the urge
to retaliate & some

people deserve to be punished.
That one I laughed at. I was told
to answer with agreement   or

strong denial. & I must have passed.
My report read: THE INMATE HAS LOW
PROBABILITY OF REOFFENCE.

   But a sentence is a sentence
   & now it's over a decade
with more to go & all my files

in a drawer full of other
men's histories, so many
histories. Do you know

the stories Do you know who
I am Do you understand
what I am Can I tell you?

   I'll try to sing this broken
song & summon my tribe   ones
who will one day carry me

home & damn damn I know
it's a moonshot but maybe
you'll come find me before I lose

myself in this jungle.

CONJURE SONG

featuring The Carters and Drake

On the yard, I pull up on JSTLK
& ask him, *How we rockin' this?*
He just smiles, laughs, & presses play—

> *Let it breathe.*
Let it breathe . . .

Doc,
my Dog, my Ace, my G:
help me conjure the bloom of the young
one you just delivered,
help me bring it back, way

way back to the Frank's Red Hot
on liquor store chips, the pink, tall tees
we rocked over our small wings like Killa
Cam. Then back, back when we flew over fences
toward the feral darkness, pulling out
of parking lots in your Mazda with the leather
seats & the thunder-filled trunk.

> All those nights we blew
> smoked to a stupor
> below the ashen shells
> of someone else's dream.

& you, Ray, my accomplice,

tight-lipped bulldog of a brother,

help me conjure the first
track we recorded—remember that?

Remember that, bruh?

How I finished our chorus:

I will never fade away . . . .

Do not burden yourself,
but lend me some strength,
& a rucksack for my journey.

Lend me your lighter words
& freestyles that I might dazzle
a few local governors & warriors.

O brothers of my youth,
Ya'll know who I am.
I am chained & imperfect.

I am savage & made of redwater.
I speak of nation when I really mean
light, & the physics of loneliness,

the sweet tinge of blood in my mouth
as I spit the bars of another:

don't tell me that you knew it would be like this all along
I know the truth is you won't love me until I'm gone
and even then the thing that comes after is moving on

'cause, my brothers, I am so damn
charged & at a hustle to escape

the bitter regions of my body,
this dumb-hearted nation-state.

Show me the renegade warbler
for I sing of hustlers & saints.

I.

: *No guard can shut me off, no law can prevent me.*[*]

: *My voice goes after what my eyes cannot reach. . .*[†]

: *I don't have a unit of measure for what this does to the heart.*[‡]

: *It was my way of breaking free. I was anything but history.*
I was the wind.[§]

[*] Walt Whitman, "Song of Myself," sec. 33
[†] Walt Whitman, "Song of Myself," sec. 25
[‡] Naomi Cohn, "Cell"
[§] Joy Harjo, "Running"

NOTES FOR IF I FADE AWAY

Brownout '03

*featuring Robert Hass, Kendrick Lamar Duckworth, and Sean "JAY-Z"
Carter*

This is to remind you that I loved you
way back. You, with your sleepless
rivers & strings of power lines—titans
gathered into formations of tender
flesh & luminous pleasures. You
are always moving. *Longing, we say,*
because desire is full of endless distances.
An apartment building. Two boys, different
shades of brown. Sun above, acting
as father. Prayer as two fists arcing—brown
boy with good hair choked by the parentheses
of his shoulders—broken horse. Please don't
mistake these notes for elegies. *These are the breaks,*
the summer where I learned of hunger & the absence
of pain. Bridgewater, that slagheap
hooptee moored in our oak-ridden suburbs. Glimmers
of future lives. Sashabaw, Dixie, Maybee Road. Loose change for 75 cent coneys.
          The big homies
pushing bags behind the skate park—all the white
paint peeling off the divider wall. The chain-link
fence we tore back, between our cracked pavement
& the fairway. The brownout that melted five
days—how I dipped my feather-light body
in the tub to keep cool. The water
searching me like so many soft lights. The general
mind was hollow back then & I did as I do now.
I sketched your patterns into the margins
of my ribs. This was before "Meet me
at the corner wash" or "your turn to go

to the Marathon" became slang for the lies
we believed. Before the 3 a.m. streetlights,
the palms crowded with earthtones. Before I learned
logic & before we should've read *Hamlet:*
Lord, we know who we are yet we know not what
we may be. Where I learned to be in the middle
of bright islands & dimebags. Those whisper-filled trees,
the pavement begging to kiss my knees.

SOPHOMORE HOMECOMING

We drove three hours up north to hit
a grow house our rich friend put us up on,
wanting to be down & spilling
tributes into our thirsty mouths. Five
kids in a pick-up, three guns, one jagged
plan. Miles into the woods, we crept
over dead leaves. Cinder block
through the mark's car window to draw
him out of his trailer. "Hello? Hey!
Who's out there?" We had plans
to keep it smooth but Ray pulls the hammer
back on the borrowed revolver, a trillion
trees cracking in the night. Now holed
up in his spot, our mark floodlights
the clearing. Last thing he probably saw
was the glint of a pistol
& five hoodies hung over bird bodies
running like dogs into dark.

ONTOLOGY OF GOD

featuring a line by Maya Marshall

Big Mike says "I read that dogs
don't have a sense of time"   a minute
is like an hour an hour like a day
          a day like a minute. The continuity

is skewed & time is placed without
thought into various boxes. I think
what it must be like to be
a dog because   yes   I be

with my dogs in this massive cage
            trying to exhaust every thread
of thought surrounding time. Maybe
that's why we say things like *Oh, [name]?*

Yeah that's my dawg & use *dog*
as a placeholder for when we secret
the names of those involved
            in the robbery stabbing   extortion.

        We want to shake off the slough
of our numbered bodies   hieroglyphs
            in our skin sluiced onto the floor.
We want to live in a space

free of calendars & clocks & the minutes
        we must share   but the high
fruits are not ready to fall from this
 life. Not yet. Ciph & Civ claim Godbody

& who am I to tell them otherwise
        when we all want to claim
master   key to lock   silo to grain
& again own the contents

of our own duffle bags & spoken
languages without restraint. Still
when I call Doc he says "What's good
God?" & tells me about my god-

daughter   her mews & her small body
taking hold of the world around
        her. When I buried my faith
I didn't dig deep   no   I didn't

& from the dirt sprung forth a woman
I asked her   "What is your name?"
& she just smiled past me   which left
me confused and shouting across the void:

What good is a god you can't trust?
When I woke up I broke bread
with my dogs. Prisms of light escaped
the prisons of our now godly mouths.

BODIES OF WATER

There are no empty vessels when everything has proper weight.
—James Wood

Sitting in the substance abuse class we talk
about moderation. The therapist
            loosens the clenched jaw each man

has labored for years to claim as his own,
                        opening the floor to the stories we
claim. The watchwords are *criminal thinking*

& this is commonplace. This is everyday
in the joint   correction. That's what this is:
            correction   correction in the depart-

ment of closely governed boxes. Bodies
of water are different   no longer
signified in themselves   but   these   bursting

symbols   overflowing with money &
drugs & the women we see in photo-
copied porn. They become our desires,

transposed among the pasts we had assumed
to be ours. Stories we lived in real time
            yet are read fast by this institution

as empty   vessels to be filled
& tossed long into whatever ocean
borders the nation with the most bullets

& the most mechanisms to keep us
from loading those bullets. We are thirsty
for any other ocean   for bodies

of water   not   weighted with the remnants
of these floating cages   of correction
        of anything unseen   but still policed.

HE SAYS HE'S MADDECENT/THE VAPORS (JSTLKMVMT REMIX)

featuring Cam'ron and the Diplomats, Drake, Hey, Arnold!, Rick Ross and Meek Mill, Kendrick Lamar, and XXXTentacion

I want you
to think about me, *tell your friends about me*
& when I say *you* I know now that *you*
                 means something different
to each of you that reads
                 this here.

But the you who
I really mean is the you
who should know that you're all
that matters here.

I hope you see that now.
(I really mean it.)

·VANDALS & WAVES·

ah baby, I just wanna / make chakra music
for all days / tryna be fire / for you
                 (you know?)
always thought / I was sayin' that / always did
                 (even back then)
hopped up on / dopeboy vernacular / all in my mouth
like liquor on a riptide / left-handed pass-off
flock'a beach chair vandals / sandals & Nikes / tryna make noise
coulda been rude boys / (manners was too tight)
woop woop woop / stoop kid's afraid
to leave his stoop / we used to clown
no joke: / five dealers crammed / up in a Jetta

faithful sing-along / T-Swift / subwoofer masseuse
hard-shell tacos / madlove junkies
when that hotline bling / & that's
the misused trouble / with knowing things

·PORN·

don't be off-
ended I can't
          help it these days, besides
I've never been able to desire
          anything simply. gift
& curse (blueprint). & now

I want you
on my tongue at the most improper
          times: while you're on
lunch break, immediately
following a run,
right before
          you go to work, while you Skype
          your friends, even if I was free.

          sometimes I just want a soft ass
to grip, two lips to brush with my own,
to lap up as if all days were desert,
          & they were my water, only mine.

sometimes I want to be held down,
released from the trap of American manhood.

          I rub out
the inevitable words on this paper
& try to take hold
          of all this gorgeous energy

but it's not enough,
        it's never enough so I jerk
        off & god
it's cheap, that fraudulent reduction.
sometimes I imagine my heatwave
laying a blanket over many states.

my goal here is to question
the domination
of the vapors that form me,
that is, my goal is to not
have a goal,

just a rich laughter full of wax
& wane
& want
& whine.

·DRUGDEALER SEASONS·

used to like getting fucked up
on a blacksky rant & rave & find
something to love 'til death. not exactly
convinced of what's changed: something or
the something? when I was a coke dealer
I snorted all the profits with G.
then I snorted the rest with G
because life back then was just a perked up
process of forgetting tomorrow. I wanted
her, but we would just drive around
while I kept up the impressions, & she counted
the money, & we blew doozeys off textbooks
in the shelter of interchangeable driveways.
predictably, my love of summer ether'd out.

then, two years later: the breakfast nook in October.
one green plastic lime, one bottle
of José Gold. My girl's mother sipping
craft beer & washing crusty dishes,
churching about random pieces
of facts. Sarah's face would bloom bright pink.
the whole scene sunk into claustrophobia.
I'd get dumbflooded with maddreams then get real
restless. I believe in picking up loose change.
I can say with degrees of certainty I dropped
these bright creatures (or was it you?). funny tricks
they're glued to the sidewalk or embedded in the Earth.

·OLD SCHOOL RECOUNTS THE RADIO/
NOTICE OF LETTER OF REJECTIONS (REMIX)·

woke up. radio:
　　　"Give yourself
　　　permission."
　　　never reveals
for what. I don't know
　　　I never
　　　　seem
　　　　to know
still these folks are damn
　　　　insistent: "permission
　　　allows you
　　　a freedom
like nothing else."
　　　Steve Harvey
　　　& his commercial ass
　　　mustache.

You have received mail containing:
excessive paperwork—origami ghosts.
Prisoners are prohibited from receiving
sparks that may pose a threat
to the security, good order, or discipline
of the facility; may facilitate or encourage
stepping off the line; or may other-
wise cause static in the civilization
of the prisoner.
Letter cannot be
easily searched
due to volume (poses
diffuse custody & security
concerns).

[poets screamin' "gang gang" /
my mail still gettin' checked]

·SOMEWHERE IT BREATHES·

An older couple dancing in their kitchen; Anita Baker turned up high. She floats through the rafters, and they dance and dance and think about the Ford Motor days. The clarity wrenches absolute and I wonder how institutionalized I really am. This scene is happening simultaneously all north and south of my hometown.

There is a man inside the devastating hour and no one asks where he's headed. Miles Davis saunters vast, wide in his head. He's touching all corners, smoothing the mad circuit, one would think. And I wonder: *the vapors?* I'm turning lofty. Distilled bliss staggers down the lonely avenue and we all rush to ask what it might mean.

·FUTURE FRAGMENTS (YOU & I)·

chocolate wrapper
on the night-
       stand
       canvas / capillary / collarbone
paint   flow
       crumpled
       sheet

       Musiq / music
flame
       dance / rain
dance
       candle wax
       streetlight / shadows / whisper
       something / something / those years
       lift / lay / rising tide
gravitybender
       vandal / vapors / vibrate

·YOU (YOU)·

if there's any
thing breathing
I've met it
in history or you
or dank nights
on the lake (the fire
dancing
into the ripples
& slices). the wet
grass at three
AM, the shaking chain
links were once
my lovers. I wanna
shake you up maddays
into the night,
you, *look at me,*
look at me
YUH—
I'm young with just
the right amount
of fire, that
rugged sophistication
you can feel
in your throat
don't you want me
I once
thought words
were for beings
of light work, I still
think so in times
like you wading
in this fucking

sea of verbs,
seems like I
can't do any
thing in
true
form.
I drink my coffee
raw in want
of—
I get choked
up when I
see people eat
alone,
it kills me
& I'm filled
with raucous stories
apparently unspooled for you
in all the rampant
lights
all seasons.
I've never been so charged
up in my life, no one
has ever seen me
this way, this
body
full of practice.
I may have lost sight
of the different notes
between the two forms
of novel
but so what
levitate
levitate
levitate
levitate
the kid grew

to thrive on you,
your complexities.
I was taught
to make conjectures:
if I could fuck you
into showing up late
to engagements, I would
& wouldn't

apologize, never
for a heated shiver, all
in all
I'm a [mad]decent
guy, juxtaposition
or proof? still
what if the whole
of our worlds
were bunk voodoo
to the universe
enveloping us.
I'd like to avoid any
brand of inventory-taking
so I breathe
in the vapors
& make it
a practice
&
addiction.

: You have come to shore. There are no instructions.[*]

: It's like a jungle sometimes.[†]

[*] Denise Levertov, "The Book without Words"
[†] Grandmaster Flash & the Furious Five, "The Message"

YOU MUST LEARN TO CLIMB

after Patrick Rosal's "Ode to Eating a Pomegranate in Brooklyn"

Since I have fallen in love again, I have sprouted
new limbs which I allow to sway

from the windows of my cell & a molt
of a tongue that gets down & pearls

each blessed word I wrap in skin & send
into my beloved, this is a simple yet gorgeous method

for growing fruits & eating them too,
   watching the seeds fall to the soil

when fingertips slip & flowers
   sprout like islands

Since I've fallen in love again, I've bled
magic from the world which holds me & ciphered

the story I've been given: while resting upon a blade
of grass I noticed volumes on volumes of books

scattered around me, I stole them all

I thieved each syllable as trees towered around me
I bartered broken prayers for rainwater

& laughed when told to bow
   toward the setting sun

I come from a line of men who stacked pennies,
harvesting coconuts from the sky

One can find light in the darkest of groves,

you just need a mouth big enough to stash shadows
This is what love does: you climb the tallest tree

only to discover a sky so wide you swear
                    no word could contain it

then you jump & you fall
                    until a song ascends to lift you

Since I have fallen again, I've pirated
one tongue & floated on my beloved's

who sings to me, *It is time*   *to come home*

ODE TO THE DOZENS
ENDING WITH ME & MY DOGS

featuring Redman & Method Man

I ask Big Mike where the phrase found its life,
where the Dozens comes from, & he says
something about old firing squads
with their rifles & only one bullet
amongst the twelve possibilities.
The Dirty Dozens, he says, & I proceed
to roast S-Dot like,

    You ol' I'm-thirty-six-
but-I'm-wearin'-a-shirt-made-for-a-six-year-old-
lookin' mawfucka! & on & on
because can't nothing stop us when we play
the Dozens. Mone X chiming in
like, *Get 'em!* Now add Civ & Ciph
Tarzan, Will, JR, Big Mike & we roast
one another like,

    You ol' prison-Under-Armour
commercial-lookin' mawfucka!
    You ol' lookin'-like-I-wear
a-twelve-but-really-I-rock-a-six-and-a-half-
lookin' mawfucka!
    You ol' "I'm the captain now"-
lookin' mawfucka!
    You ol' WHAT ARE THOSE?!-
lookin' mawfucka! & it's like family talk,
it's like Saturday morning in the sun
off the OJ & vodka to numb the aches.

I'll take this everyday 'til I'm free.

Picture this: me & my dogs giving no fucks
about who's the shooter, who's the victim

& who's got the bullet, just laughing,
barking & carrying on, shouting, *Get 'em!*
chests out like we can't be touched.

INSTITUTIONAL(IZED) ELEGY

~~Though mid-April, today could've been~~
~~the first day of summer, clear sky,~~
~~every squad on the yard, tank tops & shit,~~
~~blankets~~ ~~of~~ ~~smooth~~ ~~air,~~
~~each stereo~~ bang ~~-ing Nipsey.~~
~~Today,~~ ~~a~~ ~~man~~ ~~murdered~~ ~~a-~~
~~nother man, stabbed him in the throat,~~
~~ear & mouth in the cell they share(d).~~
~~After, I was hungry. Now, I'm just tired.~~

AT THE END OF THE DAY

A ragtag ball team
   we stand in a cipher

huddle & high five, promise to call each other's people
once released into the world & to write letters
& put money on our homies' books & some cry
& some laugh & some stay stone-faced with bangers
          in their waistbands

& we jump with our feet kicked back
in the air like the Wayans brothers in prison
   blues & we freeze-frame
   for the movie we're all in to audition for

         American History X / Prison Song
        American Me / Shawshank Redemption
         South Central / Doing Hard Time

   we don't freeze-frame for the movie
    we're all in to audition for & we don't jump
with our feet kicked back in the air
like the Wayans brothers in prison blues

        & some don't stay
stone-faced with bangers in their waistbands & some
don't laugh & some don't cry & we don't put money
on our homies' books & write letters, promise to call
each other's people once released into the world & we don't huddle & high five

we don't stand in a cipher
   a ragtag ball team

at the end of the day
truth is, we look away

OLD SCHOOL TELLS ME

Nothin' will soothe you but time. Let go

of that dream where you hover

your hands over the city and only sunbeam

laughter overflows the alleyways and death

has no place to peddle its wares. I feel you,

you wonder what it means, cancer

in the body that wove you. Listen,

Youngblood, you got to stick, you got to

move—only way this backwater

world won't beat you down. And all them variables

you think you find in the fragments. Burn 'em

to ashes and shoot them to the sky. Hell,

light 'em up in a poem to remember

where your body vibrates. The sand crane on chill

in front of your childhood home, at a slight distance

from her kind. How she refuses to sink

into the concrete and needs no abstract concept

to reflect the spring sun. The steady flow of men

in the compound where you build a world. How they fill

each room and build mass in a local organ

and carry stories from the chemicaled streets

that made them. Take all those shards,

Youngblood, and burn 'em out of you like bodies

in a killing field. Because if you don't . . .

if you don't, you'll cut yourself to pieces

and, let me tell you, a man with scars

is exactly that: a man with scars

who tends a vast field riddled

with bones and glass. Then you'll starve

because, Youngblood, there ain't no food

out there for a lover who uses his blade

to cut breath away from the starved Earth.

WARMER NOW, MICHIGAN WINTER

featuring Nas, Justin Bieber, James Baldwin, Ye, James Bay, and The Chainsmokers

·YOUNG POET SCRAPES UP GHOSTS·

lunchtime—guys look up!
into hollow atmosphere, open-mouthed, tongue
in the wind, catching intermittent
snowflakes
from a sky the color

                    dirtywater. that could be a lie (not likely)—
        Thorazine shuffle.
youhearme? youhearme?
        youhearme? fragmented shit talkin'
penguin stances with the baggy eyes out
the buttoned collars. youhearme?

                everybody's lookin' for something.

·RADIO SAYS·

"we want you
to see Adele at the Palace
in September!" it's January, don't they know
how much two seasons could explode or expose
a singular life into lapses
of osmosis, of *blueandbeige* fervor? a moment
breathes too heavily now.

            silent ambience: radio was on a timer.

·VIEW FROM WINDOW·

frozen dirt under the orange
lights, an impending trend (the pundits say). a bit of white—
        no, not the population—
the ground! distant pines bleached with midnight.
chain-link cathedral.

       lately feelin' like a needle in a dank haystack.

·INTERLUDE·

      cell activities on loop
      or maybe time-lapse? Stone hopped on
the upstate ride then S-Dot brought the radio,
          new clientele,
          nail clippers to stash the makeshift motor.
excess pop music.
is it too late now
to say sorry? *Love & Hip Hop*
effervescent. Kardashians in full bloom.
      I'm burning here, drifting probably.

                get a letter read
                a letter drop the daily
                one week two
                 week
                pour, sift, pour, *what*
               you writin' a novel? I'm
                 not sure anymore.
                every
                thing's
                 magnified.

light start new year. frequence
in laughter now—*high-five!*

(look at the elbow, it's the road to perfection.)
(gotta make 'em laugh.)
S-Dot & I in the cell. moonwalk with the wagging fingers, doing the jig
for no reason, goofystyle behind steel
and cinderblock nights.

                suspension of half-hearted
                resolutions. *I'll be better tomorrow.*
                ARF! when we reverberate and Oakland County vibrates
slowly behind while still

somewhere in the quickly aging distance.

        thou knowest this man's fall, but thou knowest not his wrassling.

·ELSEWHERE·

gin and tonics foreshadow the Uber
downtown. immaculate tears
in ancient church
shadow. party brunch: Sunday
funday in the warmer now D.
phone call: *I just need to be fucked
senseless*—vicarious afternoon to say
the least.
rented spot
in Ferndale right
on the urban cuff, a fringe
we all cling to. molly
at the afterhours. rage go dumb
stumble out
go numb. high school

        friend pocketed education (fully paid for!) new
          data analyst. see? things
         sometimes do happen. back in hometown
        our young ghosts parade through

the old stomping grounds
dope migration.
reverse urban flight.

somehow, we keep waking up in strange rooms.

·HERE·

encounter on the scene:
yellow meets self while
self falls hard,
that's what self
supposes. colorblast implodes sky,
once-hidden voice suggests.
and yesterday guy
says America's being poisoned
becoming feminine, gay,
and black. I can't help
but think *manifest*
destiny? green grass
never died was just once covered,
dirty snow, and boot prints.
(*youhearme?*) no one 'round here

seems to care just ache
for drink and fuck and eat
and sleep.
a couple hard-nosed cats
flippin' cards for white soaps, ramen blocks.
they hear there's a new whiteboy
with a few daddy issues conveniently
they got a history of problem
solvin'. kid next door drunk
off potato liquor (his own party brunch):
scraping sandals when he walks,

head hung low like a Creek man
along the grudge-march to the great
American West, says he's part
Native. *true story.* I guess
all our histories are dyed
or stained. and in strange innocence to boot.

Man, I promise, I'm so self-conscious.

·GANGS·

bloods crips vice
lords gangster
disciples latin kings
and counts
spanish g's
and cobras
insane prefixes
godbodies (*son*)
religious affiliations
euros and honkeys
three-one-three letter
crews bike clubs
north south east west
reppin' time (*youhearme?*)
recruitment season early
for the summer treaties

you tryin' to come home?

·YOUNG POET DREAMS A FUTURE WITH HER·

red eye
west coast

looking around
for early
morning antidotes.
midpoint between
motherland fatherland

all fairweather
excuses
lone reason. . .
who you kiddin'?
wore it on your sleeve, kid.
well, I'm not howlin'
no regional blues.
(how often does this happen?)
just let it be.

"... WINS FELLOWSHIP...
HOLISTICALLY FOR LIFESTYLE...BRILLIANT
PROJECTS UNDERWAY. . ."
always knew he'd make it. . . always
knew.
could one day be
well-structured puzzle
piece in Oakland, Frisco.

woke up on the far side of the spectrum.

·ROSES·

trying to hide away
they keep trying
to civilize me.

say you'll never let me go.

·SITDOWN·

Marvin listener.
come-hither breeze slips
inside open window. nothing
so clear as the ardent
stretch. many
a koan soothed
with this chanting
of the trenchant sun.

> *decided on the playground we all wanted new flavors.*

·Q&A·

Mr. Bureauman, how much time can money buy?

...

Mr. Troubleman, when innocence shifts, where does it go?

...

> *a warm front came and went. puddles,*
> *puddles all around, early under the rising*
> *light.*

AMERICAN INMATE

featuring Meek Mill

Inmate in cuffs, Inmate in curls. Inmate born in a
small world. Inmate goes to prom with neighbor.
Inmate tweets about it later. Inmate bleeds from cut
from shave. Inmate in time-out: "You've
misbehaved." Inmate raves. Inmate craves. Inmate
studies for good grades. Inmate of number, not of
name. Inmate in race for power, fame. Inmate
quotes Lupe Fiasco. Inmate eats their eggs with
Tabasco. Inmate falls asleep before The End.
Inmate drives to mall with friends. Inmate holding
jury instructions. Inmate still working in
construction. Inmate with son. Inmate with gun.
Inmate on vacation. Inmate on run. Inmate
drowning in student loans. Inmate needs second
mortgage on home. Inmate so tired of being alone.
Inmate sits down to pen a poem. Inmate in house.
Inmate in cell. Inmate has cancer. Inmate gets well.
Inmate fights. Inmate writes. Inmate daydreams
late at night. Inmate kisses. Inmate fucks. Inmate
seems to have bad luck. Inmate doesn't say it
much, but Inmate thinks, *I've had enough...* Inmate
with baby growing inside. Inmate pleading, "It's not
mine!" Inmate saving to retire. Inmate with a soul
on fire. Inmate with body tight & young. Inmate
waits in line for gum. Inmate injured by contact
sports. Inmate mows the lawn in jorts. Inmate in
love and—yes!—loved back. Inmate killed while
driving black. Inmate longing for commitment.
Inmate begs for reduced sentence. Inmate in prison
(worst degree?). Inmate wonders, *What is*

free?

III.

: You've got to tell the world how to treat you.[*]

*: But you have to remember the name
they gave you first. The one you came with.*[†]

[*] James Baldwin, *A Rap on Race*
[†] Patrick Rosal, "Brooklyn Antediluvian"

NOTES FOR IF I FADE AWAY

Missing Me

after Gabrielle Calvocoressi's "Hammond B3 Organ Cistern"

When my ex sends a letter, bless her
madly. I am in a winter funk, a lull
of hard hours where I should be weaving
magic, & by now, you should know
of my addiction to hot coals
& coffee. It will kill me one day.

Just last night I tossed around in bed
unable to sleep. When I read her letter it is
ordinary & full of light. Her love
is controlling, her family alive. & silence
is what she'll give, in all likelihood, for another
& then another year. But really though?
It's all good, it's one hundred. There are too many days
when the magic hides from me. Too many days
I wander around with boots on
& too many layers, wondering if I should quit.

There are mad days I don't want to die but think of death.

I haven't yet learned to be lonely
& when an ex of mine says she misses me
my heart throws a motherfuckin' party & goddamn
if I don't bring in the trumpets like Rick James.
Missing me is like a steaming pot of rice,
with braised beef & tomato stock, for prideful bones,
& more coffee—yup! always more coffee—to wake
the parts of me that have buried themselves.

Celebrations, there should be—bonfires & ragers
for every day we welcome. Feel the 808 rumble
& the lily-like verbs that are your living friends
shouting over the highest fences & into this jungle:

We're still here!

INSTITUTIONAL(IZED) BREAK-UP POEM CONSIDERING ANOTHER DEAR JOHN LETTER AFTER I ASK MY EX HOW IT FELT WHEN I LEFT & SHE TELLS ME "LIKE YOU DIED BUT WERE STILL ALIVE" & DREAMS OF NEAR-DEATH FLOOD ME

The only time I've felt the soft kiss
of any form of death was in a car
accident which   so damn ordinary

ordinary enough to almost be
overlooked among all the possible
deaths within the daily rise-&-grind

we like to call *today*   & then today
I remembered the collision   Damn
it feels so intimate now   the split

seconds of the sharp left in which I let go
of any question of whether he would shoot
the gap through oncoming traffic & instead

of watching the pickup truck crumple
his car   I turned away   I turned my gaze
forward   I accepted the clap of metal

on metal only feet in front of me
I shattered   the passenger window
with my face & as expected   then came

the darkness we talk about but can't really
grasp   like fish speaking of space two layers
of clouded air & blue light to separate

the cracks & crevasses of the strangely known
        I heard him call me from very far away
        I heard him scream my name   my body

        beginning to learn itself   once again   blood
flooding each muscle & then the sum
of the space I held as a teenager

locking up   my body a jaw clenched
        yet trying not to shatter   & my name
again & again the whine of my name

pouring into some part of me   opening
        my eyes I saw my lap full of blood
        seatbelt taut against my leant torso

All I could say all I could say was *Fuck*
        the red dripping down my face   I heard him
breathe out & say *I thought you were dead*   *I*

thought I killed you & the weighted world crept
back into the periphery   totaled
two-door on Dixie Highway   sirens cutting

through the air   the ordinary form
of woken living settling   back
into the normalcy of afternoon

light   after none of the empty boundaries
        between myself & being every-
thing lived as boundaries   but as doors

I could open & shut in a furnished
house   home in which I sit on the floor.   still
hearing my name called   over   & over

NOTES FOR IF I FADE AWAY

For Your Future Daughters

Tell them—inside the language
of night—Trip's story. How he downed
bottles of rotgut to build a free morning, unshackled
inside a massive cage, a captive
King. The dewy grass, soaked & rotted wood
of every picnic table in sight, ragtag gang
formations under the morning lights. Please
tell them how Trip slurred a Thursday
to make-believe he had stumbled home—back
to that country called Grandville Ave.
yet stayed tightly held inside these fences
we share, brought damn near tears
telling a lifer about this cold network, which has grown
reckless to be the father of all these lost
men. *All they know is Daddy*, he said
& so the threads of home weave inward
& like clockwork we return to our Patriarch.
Tell them how everyone & no one knew
Trip had stabbed another boy & the panoptic lenses
collected each moment, how his warm hand held
a glint of steel—sharpened down to six inches
of hard desire—& how the soft skin of a cheek
accents like a comma in a long love poem, when a banger
thrusts above an open mouth—each stab a secret
as intimate as Adam's finger reaching toward
God or lips pressing your temple, your lover's tongue
tracing your inner thigh. Tell them some bodies
die over this—the closeness of open skin
& how there always flows another stanza
somewhere. How Trip was cuffed & stripped
& sent to the hole—& how Civ fell under contrived suicide
watch after he adopted a rap for the hot steel, weeks before

being released to the echoes of Glenwood & Webber.
Tell them how blood & steel & longing
& all those avenues & streets compose a music
of endless search that trickles down like rain
upon the edge of our world & its religion
of warm flesh.

INSTITUTIONAL(IZED) PASTORAL

after Ocean Vuong's "Seventh Circle of Earth"

~~wood benches~~[1]
~~caged yard~~[2]
~~barbed fences~~[3]
~~cameras / guards~~[4]
need
~~I say more~~[5]

1. Afternoon in mid-May / a squad of Eastside goons / on some politic shit / choppin' it up / about their dog, who broke / the cardinal rule / of the G Code: / he went to the police / after someone snatched / his TV. & now / consequences must trail

2. close behind the loose- / lipped sin. They watchdog / circle the yard, beg / for support, & plead his / useless / case to anybody / with backers & bangers / but: Nah, ain't nobody / 'bout to save you, bruh, you know

3. what it is. & dog knows / the game, but real talk / he's a pup / only two years in on a dime / & he's just buying time / from the street governors / & soldiers linked by sentences / & treaties. He looks past the fences & remembers / the weight of his old pistol.

4. & he can't check into PC / 'cause after two weeks / Administration would throw him right back to the wolves / & besides, he's got too many years / left to keep hidin'. / So when yard closes, / he's swallowed / by a crowd & a squad moves / to box him in before / the cameras record / their faces

5. & just before he's trapped / look how broken he is / to be a body / & still no one / at all.

EDUCATION

featuring Method Man

We were sitting in the mentoring class
—freshly revamped, new roughnecks to kick it
with—when a man from my table named Los
was called on to stand & read a passage
on self-esteem & Los said, Nah, I'm good,
which was taken & volleyed back & forth
between Los & Walt, who supervises
us mentors & can't help but goon up
from time-to-time, until Los confessed
that he can't read. God, I wish you were there.
I wish you could have witnessed the stoic
faces of these thirty-six muscled men
in their state-blues, in their beards & their locks
& fades, when Los locked his eyes to the floor
& the men became a chorus of gods
code-switching the Dozens into a free-
style of madlove. First, one brother says, Ay
we got you homie, then another, Yuh,
you good, it ain't shit, & then Civ offers
to read for him, but Walt doesn't relent.
He directs another mentor to help
& signs Los up for a reading workshop.
I wish you could have witnessed this *ruggedraw*
kickin' down ya goddam door
group of hustlers & hardnoses after
Los stumbled on through that foreign passage,
the applause almost bursting through the seams
of that prison classroom, the subtle smirk
Los rocked as he sat down, tiny droplets
of sweat rolling gently below his braids.

OLD SCHOOL TELLS ME

Watch them fields out there
how they sit barren and flat
and in months they'll explode upward
and hide the house in green

The silver concertina
coiled all around us, the men
movin' in ciphers and circles
sights held down to pavement
or lifted up to the sky

and on the softball diamond
in puddles of rainwater
an infinite stretch of blue
and high, high up, the jet streams
connect all the cirrus thrones

Youngblood, one day you gon' learn
don't nothin' end, everything
just restarts, including you—

6 A.M. IN FREELAND, OR
LISTENING TO "EVERYBODY DIES" IN THE
DAY ROOM WITH A DECADE LEFT ON MY BID

Almost every man I know talks too goddamn much. All my favorite poets are women & gods. What I really miss is the pavement at midnight, my elongated shadow. There are mornings when the hunger pulses through me, when I just want to see a man die like an ox in a flooded field, where every witness is swallowed at once by a minute of silence, then continues the work of living. It's not that I'm thirsty for blood. I just want to be alone & with you at the same time. G told me long ago she thinks I'm cold & I responded for years by writing on shreds of paper, *my mind is on fire*. She slipped them into her mouth & waited for the wet grass of a man she could love. On my sternum there is a thumbprint from where you pressed a seed into earth. G told me, *to be us is to die*, before we kissed on the hood of my car. I charged up & doubled down against my own death. Years ago, I stole the knives necessary to bleed my idols & I haven't stopped drinking since that first cut. They're buried in my garden now, whispering into each other's ears, fingers wet with blood & water, combing through your hair. Two suns live behind my eyes & while one rises, the other sets.

LOOK AT THIS LINE:

featuring JAY-Z

<--->

It is straight. It is clear & marked. It may be the horizon or the end touches of a high fade. It may be the timeline upon which you dot your collected images, forming the thread of your life's logic. It may be the line by which you are monitored and recorded. It may be the line by which you are investigated for drug dealing. They might call it a line of inquiry, or of trafficking, though, like the timeline, only a strand is formed. The body is more than its edges. In theory, the line may go on forever. In practice, you know all things must reach a terminus—most likely an intersecting line. It is ambiguous, the line, but also synecdochic. As in: It is a component of a box, should you multiply it in space. This may happen when the line is crossed, knowingly or otherwise. In that way, the line is a boundary—a border. You may walk the borderlands while listening to HOV preach: *Nothing real can be threatened, nothing unreal exists.* You were taught to laugh like a dog at the line. You may try to toe the line but, like you know the pen is only as mighty as the fist clenched around its hollow body, you know you were bred to cross it. And thus—look at the line—the contraction of the box invades your body like a curse, and the expansion of the borderlands maps itself as something not unlike a crooked psalm: *Should my sins go unforgiven, let this language go unerased.*

THE JUDGE TOLD ME,
"YOU SEEM TO DO BETTER IN CHAINS"

Every angel

I've ever met had clipped wings
& two mouths, one to spit bullets,
one to swallow the spent casings.

America wove me this way: to taste of sweetness
then to orchid on the tongue with dirt
& blood, to hide my gold threads

in plain sight, & bare my skin
in warmth, did she not? I learned
her like that, braille on my rough finger-

tips: the opposite of emptiness & still
a cartridge for flowers. So many
flowers. On the day of judgement, he saw just one

echoed angle of my desire. I wanted her to make me
a brute, a hellish creature who gnaws
at his palms in the hours he is not sucking

marrow from her femur. I crowded my mornings
with this lust. Of course. When you give language
to a savage nature it will eat wild herbs

& bark until it can conjure itself
without guilt. This is how I came
to have a body living in both Heaven

& Earth. America refused to mistake
my steam for silence & I began to call

her a country, something like home. So now

when a man tells me I am fit to be jewelry
for kings, I will laugh & betray
the burns on my native tongue.

LOCKDOWN POETICS (JSTLKMVMT REMIX)

after Maged Zaher's "The Consequences of My Body"

featuring Jason Mraz and Bryson Tiller

Ciph asked me today: "So, have you put any thought into what you want to do
when you get out of here?"

*

Here in this life
We take showers
Touch ourselves
Eat fruit
& commit to letters

We dream of liquid swapping
We get off to echoes

*

A poem flits around me in sleep

A friend used to slice his wrists
To take back his story

     Now he teases himself with fermented juice
     & the perpetual threat of collapse

A stretch mark on my arm
From navigating expansion

     This city is not static
     Even as my body extends itself
     Undisclosed

*

My bones have become esoteric
Inside this royal structure
That builds pieces of our hunger

We open our mouths

Waiting for this sticky
Month to pass

We send fragments of desire
A holdover until we kiss
The pieces floating back
To our electric core

*

The men around me string together methods of living in the bareness of
            concrete & each other

They starve us of touch then ask us to be trustworthy on visits

I am preparing for an emergency shakedown

I wake into this world over & over again

*

I only play
Sports in which
I feel like I might take off
& fly.

In recent years,
I've conjured an airport,
A lift-off point

Where I may rub ripples

Into the thick ground

While we perform
Tiny murders
Of mathematical inefficiencies.

        *

Between death & sometime soon
I find my body between sentences
Sitting in rooms
Without rest from functional architecture,
Warmer now again
      Inside a square mile

      Absent the internet.
My body gathers under
Pressure in the immediate
World.

      *

We spoke on the phone today for the first time—we've been in love for six months, give or take a year—do you want me to call again? Should I?—I did—not ten minutes after we both said, *I love you & bye*—I wanted to tell you something I ended up sending in a message—but still. . .—Maybe I just need to know your voice is coming from hundreds of miles to speak with me—you comfort me in a city where comfort comes with hidden costs—forreal—& now I'm tripping about your next message—wondering if you'll fall back—wondering if you think I'm too thirsty—because when I called back to tell you about infinity (the future, the past, everything in between) or whatever I would have spilled or went on about—you didn't answer—So, I wonder if you didn't want to kick it with me again, yet—or maybe you did? Maybe you saw my name under *Missed Calls* & felt anxious?—Are we both on edge now?—Is this what madlove & bondage does to young poets?—I'm still navigating this—how to respect the distance while showing you that we can cross the void, somehow— How far am I going when I say, *I'm yours & you're everything*?—I'm just being real—You're all I think about—& now, are you thinking of us like I am?—I've got to go, I need a shower—I'll beg the water to drip down my back

*

Wondering if we think about similar things before we go to sleep—right now in different parts of this vast country on the brink of madness

*

I drink coffee & atomize my body into layered
Script

I feed the soft machinery
Electricity & language
Both of which are pocketed

Away into hidden pores

We siphon a lunacy found in the institution
In order to tease out a few coefficients

We grow used to hard edges

A derivative drenches our bodies apart

I'm talking here about loneliness
& the way our poetics has magnetized me

*

The compound is entrenched with gangs
You can see them in each wall

While forgetting touch

My body is hungry
From remembrance
Your hand in my lap
&—incredibly—seasons still fly
& I am able to be convinced
Another world still holds me

*

When another breathes on your stomach
I am not present & I am reminded
Of the crimes I committed & the cage around me

My hands buried in pregnant thoughts of you

*

All of my poems
Have faded away

Into the swollen humidity
Of July—all clouds

Renegade verbs?
Unsung forms?

Let them sing
Let us join them

*

Old School stood there

His religious gold fronts

His balloon eyes

What's a decade
To
A natural
Life?

*

While men I know pray well
To Father God, I look around
To the world & the sky,
All of the colliding beauty
& find a woman
Whispering heat into tomato
Plants in the garden dripping
Light across strands of man-
Made metals & I get charged seeing
Gods this way, as women

Not of lack but of light
& creation even inside capitalism

*

Wondering if we think about similar things before we go to sleep—right now
in different parts of this vast country on the brink of madness

*

To live within fences
Is a muffled life.
We stitch correctional patterns,
Squares inside of squares
As our younger sisters speak

Computer love

*

A lunacy darts around between the people
In the visiting room

We watch
We move
We touch
We tease
The madness
Found in the walls

*

When life gave

  Me lemons

  I drank

  The juice

Sought out the tree

  Found it bright

  & full

Planted
A peach
Tree
Beside
It

*

Slowly, softly I float away from birth

We inhabit occasionally wet fields, each other

On D-Block 234 I stretch, I collapse.

Need to dig a way from here.

It's OK to stand in front of each other naked
It's OK to open palms, parallel them, stare

        *

JR asked me today: "So, have you put any thought into what you want to do
when you get out of here?"

        *

When I die let it be with the imprint
Of our shared mornings
Of brilliance we found in seeds
Of your dance & our hands
Fluttering like birds
Over the summer's late lights

        *

I want to be
A zero
No longer

IV.

: You have to make peace with the chaos but you cannot lie.[*]

: Your life is a painting in a dark museum and sometimes you
examine it closely[†]

: (My newfound life found all of me magnified)[‡]

* Ta-Nehisi Coates, *Between the World and Me.*

† Guillaume Apollinaire, trans. by Donald Revell, "Zone"

‡ Kendrick Lamar, "FEAR."

PRAYER OF THE SQUAD

featuring J. Cole, Drake, Kendrick Lamar, Wale, and Ye

back when *a dollar & a dream* was loose
in my cargo pocket,
when Mark & I *were those kids in the basement*
(been at it before Twitter
names),

I got super lifted on that back porch
& vibed on *hiiipower,*
watched Action Jaxon & Mark the Spark
kickflip *'til infinity*
came

into the fuzzy warm periphery
(one cannot be judged
when he's dressed like his brothers
melancholy we all acted
calm

still troubled). that silver S-10
blossomed bass into the street,
the garage boomed with desire,
poured rhythm & ratchet
psalm:

laaaaaaa,
laaaaaaa,
laaa, laaa,
wait 'til I get my money right

PRE-SENTENCE INVESTIGATION (JSTLKMVMT REMIX)

from the Michigan Department of Corrections Pre-Sentence Investigation Form

We fill pre-existing forms, and when we fill them, we change and are changed.

—Frank Bidart, "Borges and I"

WHIPPING WHITE, BLACK sky. So much black and white. And then, through the blizzard, the fluorescent lamps of the coffee shop, the parking lot almost empty, the whole scene drenched in gold light. Everything around the building was glowing, almost vibrating in the snow.

WE HAD PARKED across the street from the coffee shop, in the neighborhood where my mother and brother lived. The distance between Ray's Explorer and the coffee shop wasn't far, maybe four hundred feet, but it took us ten minutes to reach the small Christmas tree lot next to the stand-alone building. On the way there, we passed a young man and woman, or at least two people I assumed to be a young man and woman—they didn't seem to carry much weight, even with the scarfs and snowsuits, and when they said, "Hi, how ya doin?" as we passed, their voices seemed too mousy and cheerful to come from adults in a blizzard—right before we crossed Maybee Road, at that point the throughline of our tribe. Snow flurried around us as we trudged across the empty road.

Attached is corrections. Contained is identification documents

and number. Some history is years old.

Years is continuing pattern as an adult forming decision.

State of seriousness.

Dangerousness is anxiety due to anxiety due to guidelines.

Employment is self having chance for system of options as a juvenile.

A range of information is the window to cash on video.

The race was blue and black and stolen.

Borrow a notebook and a gun.

Suspect #1: male of unknown race medium height & weight dark-colored hooded sweatshirt unknown writing on front orange ski goggles blue jeans white shoes dark colored gloves small black handgun

Suspect #2: male of unknown race light colored hooded sweatshirt "MICHIGAN" written on front blue in gold white framed ski goggles blue jeans white shoes long gun

Police observed the cash till on the floor. All the paper missing. Police observed footprints on the freshly mopped floor and outside in the snow. The K9 unit lost track.

ONE MINUTE, Doc and I are getting ready to go to the park with the squad. The next, I'm stuffing my clothes into a duffle bag, calling Mark to ask if I can stay with him for awhile. Then, I'm sleeping on a couch at Mark's, his mother calling me Son, sneaking lunch money into my cargo shorts while I shower, G on the other couch, staying for a few months while her family takes on home renovations after the fire. This was before Mark's mother bought a bunk bed for me to assemble in the laundry room. Before I decided my job as a cashier wasn't going to pay for school clothes or a car and neither was my fledgling drug enterprise that was the cause of my departure from home. Before I moved home after New Year's and before my grandparents found a '98 Grand Prix to let me drive after my seventeenth birthday. This was before, years later, drunk, smoking cigarettes outside of a house party, Mark and I would be talking for the first time in months, him telling me, "We're family, I got you, bro."

Police spoke to supervisor. He stated he thought it was a customer entering the store. He heard the wobble from the swinging door. He saw a dark-colored ski mask. The suspect turned and looked, holding a shotgun. The supervisor immediately jumped into the drive-thru window and outside. He stopped a vehicle: "Call 911."

Police spoke to employee, Cris. She was mopping the floor. She heard someone. She turned around. She saw a white hat with orange ski goggles pointing a pistol at her. She screamed. The suspect told her to get on her knees. Cris got on her knees, closed her eyes. Her cell phone was later recovered in the lobby. The investigating officer believed the suspects moved the cellphone to prevent police.

I LIED. I created a world in which there was a blizzard, but no, there was no blizzard, only a snowstorm that swept through for twelve hours, covering our tracks then leaving. I lied when I took the stand, too. I took the oath then sat down and told the jury I didn't do it. My lawyer, a burly Korean man with a bald head, a Kingpin-looking sort of cat, pointed out to me and, more importantly, the jury, that Mark and Dave had the same heights and builds as Ray and me, respectively. I said, "Yes, Dave and I have the same build." A middle-aged woman in the jury box touched her chin and slightly opened her mouth. I wore a tan suit over a sky-blue button-down and a striped blue and green tie, rather than my prison blues. Had they known I was serving five to twenty for a different robbery, the shit would've been over before I put my hand on the Bible. It wouldn't have mattered that Dave was a gunman in the other robbery and was earning his immunity. It wouldn't have mattered that this was the same judge and prosecutor who had seen me a year before. All they would have seen was a young dude wearing prison blues, with a criminal background. But, yes: I did it. Then, six years later, I lied.

Oakland County is in the State of Michigan.

In terms of community protection, sentencing, a weapon.

December has financial anxiety.

In the Township of Progress, the suspect was wearing closed eyes.

The suspect got up and moved to the floor.

All the currency was lost.

The small return to retrieve morning.

Christmas was living at the time of the robbery.

A message was left.

The investigation did not wish to quit.

Cris was sixteen when the offenses occurred. She was afraid, reduced her hours despite needing money. Severe anxiety caused her difficulties, hard time concentrating. She has younger siblings, lives across from the coffee shop, went to school with both J and Ray. Her family did not feel safe.

WE HAD BEEF with a group of Latinos we went to school with, cats who weren't fully gang affiliated, but who had older brothers and cousins that belonged to sets heavy in their hometowns. G told us they had been trying to cop pistols from her older brother, a Latin King I had bought weed from once and only saw intermittently throughout high school. I don't even remember what the beef was over—seldom did we know or care about the reasons for the tribe flirting with young war, we just told each other it was us against the world while we got high on back porches—most likely some back-of-the-bus mean-mug shit from our middle school days, all of us getting off at the Bridgewater stop. All our conflicts were stained with that residue. Ray was the first of us to get a car, and so, the first of us to take leveling-up in the drug game seriously—other than Jaxon, his garage our infinite trap, where we watched four of the Latinos roll by slow in an old Camry—and so, especially in light of G's warning, Ray was the first to cop a pistol.

RAY AND I met up with Rich after school on a Thursday in early fall. I remember it being exceptionally bright outside, no clouds in the sky, and kids—our classmates—walking home from school, right behind the neighborhood where Rich lived. He showed us the small black pistol, a .22 snub, and Ray insisted on making sure it worked, which made Rich visibly uneasy because we had fought him and some of his boys four years prior, when we were in seventh grade and he was in eighth. The three of us walked to the practice field behind the high school and Ray fired two rounds into the air before we sprinted back to Rich's house, racing past the homes of our classmates and some of our teachers.

Dave stated he was contacted by J through Myspace. At the time, he and J were juniors. J needed a gun, would pay $100 for the use. Dave agreed. There was an unloaded .22 long rifle in the small cinder block building on his property.

Dave stated Ray drove, parked his vehicle next to the Christmas tree parking lot. Dave stated J and Ray committed the robbery close to closing time—fewer people in the restaurant. They told him not to tell anyone.

Following the robbery they had a snow day.

LATE SUMMER. THEY would have jumped us in the parking lot, stomped us out before some teachers tried to flex their authority. No question: we would've both caught the flux for his shit talking. But he never got out of G's truck. He just took two mouth shots through the open passenger window; the captain calling him a bitch while the wrestling team surrounded us. Crunched up in the fold-down seat behind him, I said, "Let's do this shit, fuck it"—the same thing Dave and I would say two years later, months after we graduated, as we planned the drug-deal robbery— but G kept pleading, "No, no it's fine, don't do it." The whole team sneered and laughed at Ray, called him a bitch again, and mobbed into the school. He was silent the whole ride back to his spot, holed himself up in his room while G and I smoked out back.

He is guilty, aggravating firearm of a juvenile, self of verified past.

The offenses were committed over five years ago.

The sentencing guidelines suggest 108 to 180 months.

The best restructuring and programming were found in a cell.

A person, pointing at the suspects lost in the snow.

The high unloaded into the morning.

The window was living.

The window provided the remains.

The victim has severe anxiety.

The defendant was revealed.

LANGUAGE CANNOT ANSWER what we ask of ourselves when we are alone. I've damaged people. I've done things that have hurt people I played basketball with, rode the bus with, walked to school with. Things I wish I could make amends for with more than my presence within these fences and a few abstract words they might never read.

Corrections your guilty.

High school was a prison of behavior involving nature.

Court criteria is very serious nature.

A certain record or evidence of history, willingness.

Subsequently, incarceration is "management."

Punishment is best.

While incarcerated, participate.

Under the dark mask, a person face, a gun.

Inside the cash was fresh snow outlined in gold, a gun.

A gun was told not to tell anyone.

A message was left.

The owner of the coffee shop requested $700.00.

The supervisor did not wish to comment.

Cris continues to experience severe anxiety.

Police spoke to Mark, who refused to answer questions. Mark submitted a statement, testified during trial.

Police spoke to Dave, who answered all questions. Dave submitted a statement, testified during trial.

Police spoke to Ray. He provided an attorney. Was found guilty, 4 to 20.

Police spoke to J. He requested an attorney. This investigation revealed no juvenile criminal history for this offender. Given the information, the best interest of the community would be served if the defendant is sentenced to the Department of Corrections. The defendant committed the offenses when he was sixteen. The defendant must be sentenced as an adult. He remains in custody, a prisoner, the other.

The honorable are guilty.

Check the documents.

The citizenship of the defendant was taken into account.

Legislation of terms including existence, other, victim.

Psychological impact caused the victim years of limited self.

This information is restructuring the defendant.

He looked up and ran toward the cell.

She was a person with face and closed eyes.

She believed in the unknown.

A long time refused to answer the offered remains.

FINALLY, WHEN YOU decide whether I have told you the truth or have lied, whether I am guilty or innocent—here there is no in-between—how can you be sure? How do you decide which stories to pull truth from like teeth, assembling a new mouth, one of delivered justice?

THIS—WHAT WE'RE doing here: you, reading; me, writing—is a trial. The page, as it lives in each of our minds, is our courtroom. I am, again, like the times in my history, the defendant. You are the judge. You are the prosecutor. Yes, you are the jury. You are my peer and, given the right beliefs, my persecutor. Of course, I represent myself, *pro se*, and will call upon my witnesses, namely myself. You will walk back and forth across the floor in your suit or conservative dress, pursuing lines of inquiry, proselytizing to the twelve yous sitting to the left of you, high up in your chair, lording over your small kingdom. You'll ask yourselves, "Can I trust this man, even after he's lied before, even after he's been convicted twice before?" Yes, I must find his guilt beyond a reasonable doubt, but what doubts have we left alive? Look me in my eyes and judge who I might become upon release, after *I was just sitting in prison damn near living like a dog.* Look at my history and ask yourself: "What kind of man do I want living next door?"

This may be your one chance to decide.

BIGTHANKS & MADLOVE

If you're reading this book, you've supported me in ways that you may not even recognize. To have your voice heard—let alone publish a whole-ass book of poems and have people listen to you—while incarcerated is a gift of immeasurable value. This collection wouldn't have been possible without the radical support of those mentioned below. I take none of the opportunities, love, or lessons I've been given for granted. Reader, without you, there is no this.

I acknowledge the institutions and organizations that helped fund the writing of this project: Kundiman, *Asian American Literary Review*, the "A Letter Mentorship" program from the Smithsonian's APAC, with the ever-brilliant Paisley Rekdal, the PEN America fam, and the Writing for Justice Fellowship that produced the first complete draft of *American Inmate*.

Madlove and solidarity to all the guys I've met on my journey through this mountainous sentence. My deepest gratitude to the CFL homies, who I expanded my mind: Mario Bueno (my forever mentor), Rick Speck, Steve "Rip" Logan, Lil Key Wilson, Camron Colts, Sidney Black, Mike Hudzick, Kassem Salamey, Ronnie and Mac, Paul D'Arcy, Big Chris, Big Ryan Belcher, Phil, Brian X, Lus Ybarra, Justis, LX, Boski, Johnny, Glen, Bino, DC, J. Marsh, Ken Gourlay, Big Vito, and all the core members and students who encouraged me and lifted me up while I was just a youngblood, stumbling and learning to lead a classroom full of men with more wisdom than me. Thank you to the Common Ground and Peer Support homies: Big O, James X, Dopeman, Speedy, Meech, Sam X, Newsome-El, Kimball-Bey, Trip Season; my fellow Delta Pioneers—Mitch, Double D, Breeze, Tay, Legal Mike, and Dunk; my main homies who done did it all with me—Tarzan, JR, and Ciph—all the inside jokes and love are waaaay too much to recount here; all the Freeland homies—Mike, Will, Green, Stone, Knowledge, Red, Lee-Bo, Base, P-Rock, Dave, Ramon X, Murder, Brightmo, Bones, Rube, Trip, OG, Capone, Phil, Joy Road, Mike Perkins, Beans, KP, Taboo-Bey, Reed-Bey, JB, Mandy, Taz C, Locs, Boom, Nutty, Conscious, my brother, Shaun. Love to all the dogs at The Lou—Ace, V, Boog, Uncle Ron, Vont'e, Haad-Money, Eddie D., Man-Man, Nato, Gordo, Brooklyn, Shawn, Running Man, Cort, and J-Stone. Shoutout to those who stand upon this Divine Foundation with me. A big shoutout to my brother, Robert "Chino" Caldwell-Kim and the whole NOTES FROM THE PEN fam—this book here is my pebble in the shoe of the Prison Industrial

Complex. Drake had it right on "Omerta": "I am just a body that my brothers are living through."

I'd like to acknowledge the prison administrators and staff who saw my potential, work ethic, and vision, who saw beyond the prison blues and lent a hand and heart, or at least allowed me to grow without too much resistance—Tim Runyan, Willie Riley, Darcy Clark, Penny Mickel (for giving your whole heart to helping men change their lives), Tia Clark (without you this book simply wouldn't exist), and Darryl Walton.

Big gratitude to the editors, first readers, general supporters, mentors, poet-friends, educators and all-around big homies who have championed my work, encouraged me, jumped through the added hoop of creating a whole JPay account to contact me, and put me on when I was in search of a poetic community—Joy Priest, J. Khadijah Abdurahman, Phil Christman and the whole Prison Creative Arts Project fam at the University of Michigan, H. L. Webster, Michael Weinstein, Joshua Bennett, Stewart Lawrence Sinclair, Kaveh Akbar, Eve L. Ewing, Cortney Lamar Charleston, Reginald Dwayne Betts (however we both may feel about the labels, you the prison-poet big homie out here for real—every writer I know with an inmate number and a pen would offer you a cook-up and the maddest respect for the road that you paved), Ryan Lee Wong, Beth Shelburne, Aja Monet, Patrick Rosal (the BIGGEST OG—I hope you know how much hope you gave a half-Filipino kid in the joint who wanted to write poems), Matt Muth, Holly Amos, John Murillo, Jonah Mixon-Webster, Alan Thomas, Srikanth Reddy, Carrie Olivia Adams, Katie Peterson, Nate Marshall, Mitchell S. Jackson, Justin Phillip Reed, Rene Verma, Kirsten Aguilar, Sean Kelley, and Rachel James at Poetry Foundation. Thank you always to Leigh, who first encouraged me, pushed me to grow, and helped me start on a path where I am a writer before a felon.

Rest in peace to my dogs—Jake Riopelle, Hubert "Young Tuck," aka "Supreme" Hoking, and Derek "Chief" Bailey.

Special shoutout to Caits Meissner, formerly the Director of the Prison and Justice Writing program at PEN America, an incredible poet, and, really, one of the biggest reasons this book is in the world. From start to finish you've been the biggest champion of this book. *Thankyouthankyouthankyou*, friend.

Wild gratitude to the whole team at Haymarket Books—Maya Marshall, Aricka Foreman, Jim Plank, Jameka Williams, and everyone involved in the production of this book. Big thanks to Sam Rodriguez for permission to use his art for the book cover.

Madlove to my day-one homies who know all the stories—Eric, Gus Scott, Jackson, Marcus, and Savannah.

To my family: words will never suffice. Mom—I would not be a fraction of the man I am today were it not for your unconditional love and guidance; I can't wait to one day take care of you like a good Filipino son. Lola and Lolo—thank you for working so hard to give us a life in this country you now call home. Dom—how did we get to a point where I'm looking up to you? So damn proud to be your *kuya*. Pops—I love you, man. Leti—thank you for always seeing the good in me. Laura, my favorite li'l soul—I miss you and love you, sis, and can't wait 'til we can kick it.

To Janice Lobo Sapigao, my love and my favorite poet: I don't know how you do what you do, but damn, baby, you DO it! Thank you for your patient, vibrant, and traveling love. My whole heart. Our small orchard. I got you, *mahal*. Shoutout and love to HGN for always carrying us. We on the way!

If I forgot you, don't be mad! It's all love over here. LOVE Y'ALL.

TERMS FOR THE UNINITIATED

AYERIGHT: initiation of call and response in the MDOC ("Ayeright... youhearme?" "Yeahhh") used to make sure inmates can hear one another when walls, doors, fences, or yards are between them.

BACKER: someone who hasn't yet "come home," or fully joined a thing, but is known as a recruit, or a prospect; if it goes up, they better be down.

BANGER: a prison shank or knife (ref. stick, tool, icepick, blicky, sword, strap); shorthand for "gangbanger."

CIPHER: a person, place, or thing; a complete circle; a group of people; a state of completion; a code to be cracked.

CRIMINAL THINKING: thought-products identified and labeled by justice systems, carceral institutions, other government entities, as antisocial, leaning toward criminal behavior, or often disagreeable to whatever lesson is being taught by a therapist within any of the abovementioned milieu.

EMERGENCY SHAKEDOWN: when the siren blows and all inmates must return to their cells to be counted, with thorough searches of bodies and cells likely to follow.

G-CODE: set of cardinal rules to be followed in neighborhoods, streets, corners, back rooms, avenues, and front streets all over the world.

GODBODY: I'll let my man Ciph DZA the God tell it: "a godbody is typically an original man who is the embodiment of knowledge, responsibility, and many other divine attributes;" a member of the Nation of Gods and Earths.

GOON-UP: to be aggressive, pull the straps out, get down to business, etc.

INSTITUTIONALIZED: when the mind has so thoroughly adapted to prison life and culture that the lines between cell-block thinking/behavior and free-world thinking/behavior become noticeably blurred.

PC: protective custody; where inmates are placed when they themselves or administration deem the yard too dangerous to be on.

PRE-SENTENCE INVESTIGATION: report generated by probation/parole officer of the Michigan Department of Corrections before an inmate is sentenced. It gives a sentencing recommendation based on a number of factors, including the history, genealogy, and prescription to a particular crime, as well as the offender. The document is used in the MDOC amongst inmates to "check their paperwork" to ensure an inmate is who they say they are, to discover if the inmate is a rat or a child molester, or to make apparent a certain subtle power held by the inmate demanding to see said paperwork (ref. PSI Party).

SEG: segregation or administrative segregation; where administration places inmates to serve time under 23–24-hour lockdown (ref. the Hole, Solitary Confinement, Laydown, the Box).

SNOWBIRD: bus used for mass transportation of inmates from Michigan's "mitten" to the Upper Peninsula—Michigan's "Upstate." MDOC inmates often get stuck once placed there.

THORAZINE SHUFFLE: extremely slow, almost penguin-like walk most used by inmates who take medication. May be used to soak up a few extra moments of time outside of the cell before lockdown (ref. Level IV Shuffle).

YARD: fenced-in area within a correctional institution where inmates workout, politic, use the phone, etc.; the general population area of a correctional institution ("dog had to get off the yard")(ref. Back-Forty).

YOUHEARME?: Michigan version of "you feel me?" "you know what I'm sayin?" etc.; part of a call and response used in the MDOC and the state of Michigan.

LINER NOTES FOR THE REAL ONES

Heavy acknowledgement to the editors, readers, and entire teams at the following publications in which these poems, some in earlier versions & forms, first appeared:

Asian American Literary Review: "You Must Learn to Climb"; "Old School Tells Me"

Blackbird: "Conjure Song"; "Ode to the Dozens Ending with Me & My Dogs"

CURA (online): "Notes for If I Fade Away (Missing Me)"

Duende: "AMERICAN INMATE"; "Warmer Now, Michigan Winter"

Hayden's Ferry Review: "Education," "Look at This Line"

Pacifica Literary Review (online): "He Says He's Maddecent/The Vapors (JSTLKMVMT remix)"; "Prayer of the Squad"

Logic: "Intro"; "Ontology of God"; "Bodies of Water"

Michigan Quarterly Review: excerpts from "Pre-Sentence Investigation (JSTLKMVMT remix)"

The Nation (online): "6 a.m. in Freeland, or Listening to 'Everybody Dies' in the Day Room with a Decade Left on my Bid" (originally published under "Everybody Dies")

The Offing: "Intro"; "Sophomore Homecoming"; "Ontology of God"; "Bodies of Water"

PEN America (online): "LOCKDOWN POETICS (JSTLKMVMT remix)"

POETRY: "Notes for if I Fade Away (Brownout '03)"; "Notes for if I Fade Away (For Your Future Daughters)"

The Rumpus: "Institutional(ized) Break-Up Poem Considering Another Dear John Letter After I Ask My Ex How It Felt When I Left & She Tells Me "Like You Died but Were Still Alive" & Dreams of Near-Death Flood Me"

"Intro" samples the Michigan Department of Corrections (MDOC) COM-PASS Assessment, a series of inquiries an inmate must answer upon admittance into the MDOC's Robert E. Egeler Reception & Guidance Center (commonly known as "Quarantine"). The COMPASS Assessment generates numerical scores for various categories, ranging from family support to criminal behavior. Results are used to determine inmate program placement, security level classification, and more. The same assessment is reviewed by the MDOC's Parole Board at the end of an inmate's minimum sentence, before a panel interview, to determine the inmate's level of rehabilitation.

"Conjure Song" samples the Carters ("SUMMER"), and Drake ("Emotionless"). The poem also evokes the moniker, "Killer Cam," of the Harlem-based rapper Cam'ron. During the early-to-mid-aughts, Cam popularized the colors pink and purple amongst male rappers, even going as hard as rocking a pink fur coat, while posing in front of his pink Range Rover. DIPSET!

"Notes for If I Fade Away (Brownout '03)" owes its life to Danez Smith's sonnet sequence "summer, somewhere." The poem samples poet Robert Hass ("[?]"), Kendrick Lamar ("DNA.") and JAY-Z ("Marcy Me"). Bridgewater is an apartment complex in Clarkston, MI, on the corner of Sashabaw and Maybee Road. Maybee Road intersects Sashabaw Road and comes to a terminus at Dixie Highway.

"Ontology of God" samples poet Maya Marshall ("I Take Myself for Walks"). My poem makes multiple uses of the terms "god" and "godbody," some of which are derived from the Nation of Gods and Earths (NGE), a cultural organization commonly known as the Five Percenters. The NGE was started in Harlem by Clarence the 13th X (known amongst the gods as Allah) after leaving the Nation of Islam. Peace to the gods!

"He Says He's Maddecent/The Vapors (JSTLKMVMT remix)" samples the Diplomats ("I Really Mean It"), the Nickelodeon TV show, Hey, Arnold!, Drake ("Hotline Bling," and "Charged Up"), Steve Harvey's Morning Show, the MDOC Notice of Letter Rejection form, Rick Ross (featured on Meek Mill's "What's Free?"), XXXTentacion ("Look at Me") and Kendrick Lamar ("Untitled 07: 2014-2016"). The poem uses the Wavytape form created by the producer/DJ/poet-editor JSTLKMVMT—a hybrid that utilizes the found-texts and build-up of impressions used in the Japanese zuihitsu (here inspired by Kimiko Hahn's *Narrow Road to the Interior*), as well as the vignettes and dynamic improvisations used in modern poetic sequences (here inspired by Walt Whitman's "Song of Myself" and Galway Kinnell's *The Book of Nightmares*). The MDOC Policy Directive covering "Prisoner Mail" (PD 04.03.118) states: "Prisoners are prohibited from receiving mail that may pose a threat to the security, good order, or the discipline of the facility, may facilitate or encourage criminal activity, or may interfere with the rehabilitation of the prisoner." Sometime around 2018 or 2019, the ad-lib/shoutout "gang gang" became popularized by Memphis rapper Black Youngsta. Needless to say, haphazardly yelling "gang gang" in certain contexts is a bad idea for those uninitiated—or, at least, not strapped.

"At the End of the Day" mentions movies that depict prison stereotypes both steeped in reality and Hollywood-packaged bullshit. Sometimes you gotta live it to feel it.

"Warmer Now, Michigan Winter" samples Nas ("Street Dreams"), Justin Bieber ("Sorry"), James Baldwin (*Notes of a Native Son*), Kanye West ("All Falls Down"), James Bay ("Let It Go") and The Chainsmokers ("Roses"). The poem makes use of the Wavytape form created by JSTLKMVMT.

"AMERICAN INMATE" mentions "Prisoner 1 & 2" by Lupe Fiasco from the album *Tetsuo & Youth*. The final line ("What is free?") comes from the Meek Mill song "What's Free" on his album, *Championships*, which he dropped after his release from prison.

"Notes for If I Fade Away (Missing Me)" owes its life to poet Gabrielle Calvocoressi's "Hammond B3 Organ Cistern." The Rick James song mentioned is "Give It to Me, Baby."

"Notes for If I Fade Away (For Your Future Daughters)" owes its life to excerpts from Reginald Dwayne Betts's groundbreaking collection of poetry, *Bastards of the Reagan Era*.

"Institutional(ized) Pastoral" owes its life to poet Ocean Vuong's "Seventh Circle of Earth."

"6 a.m. in Freeland, or Listening to 'Everybody Dies' in the Day Room with a Decade Left on My Bid" mentions J. Cole's "Everybody Dies."

"Look at This Line:" samples JAY-Z (featured on Pusha T's "Drug Dealers Anonymous").

The title "The Judge Told Me, 'You Seem to Do Better in Chains'" is based on a statement made by the judge who sentenced me. After looking through my various letters of recommendation and good character, he said something closer to: "I recognize all the good you've been doing while in there, but it seems to me that you do better when you're locked up than when you're free."

"LOCKDOWN POETICS (JSTLKMVMT remix)" owes its life to excerpts from Maged Zaher's breathtakingly intimate collection of poetry, *The Consequences of My Body*.

"Prayer of the Squad" samples J. Cole ("Dollar & a Dream (Part III)"), Drake ("0 to 100 / The Catch-Up"), Kendrick Lamar ("Hiiipower"), Wale ("Nike Boots") and Kanye West ("Can't Tell Me Nothing"). The poem makes use of the Bassment Blues form created by JSTLKMVMT and named by the incredible poet/writer/educator, Janice Lobo Sapigao.

"Pre-Sentence Investigation (JSTLKMVMT remix)" samples the MDOC (Pre-Sentence Investigation Report for Justin Monson #803755) and Lil Baby ("Humble"). The poem makes use of the Vapor remix form created by JSTLK-MVMT—a hybrid form that utilizes both prose and erasure poetics to explore the narrative potential of prose poetry. The sections rendered in italics are erasures created via chopping and screwing twelve copies of my Pre-Sentence Investigations.

ABOUT THE AUTHOR

JUSTIN ROVILLOS MONSON, a Filipino American poet & writer, was an inaugural PEN America Writing for Justice fellow and a recipient of the Kundiman / Asian American Literary Review / Smithsonian Asian Pacific American Center A Lettre Mentorship in poetry. His work has appeared in *POETRY*, *The Rumpus*, *The Nation*, and elsewhere. He is currently serving a sentence in the Michigan Department of Corrections from which he hopes to be released in 2027.

ABOUT HAYMARKET BOOKS

Haymarket Books is a radical, independent, nonprofit book publisher based in Chicago. Our mission is to publish books that contribute to struggles for social and economic justice. We strive to make our books a vibrant and organic part of social movements and the education and development of a critical, engaged, and internationalist Left.

We take inspiration and courage from our namesakes, the Haymarket Martyrs, who gave their lives fighting for a better world. Their 1886 struggle for the eight-hour day—which gave us May Day, the international workers' holiday—reminds workers around the world that ordinary people can organize and struggle for their own liberation. These struggles—against oppression, exploitation, environmental devastation, and war—continue today across the globe.

Since our founding in 2001, Haymarket has published more than nine hundred titles. Radically independent, we seek to drive a wedge into the risk-averse world of corporate book publishing. Our authors include Angela Y. Davis, Arundhati Roy, Keeanga-Yamahtta Taylor, Eve L. Ewing, Aja Monet, Mariame Kaba, Naomi Klein, Rebecca Solnit, Olúfẹ́mi O. Táíwò, Mohammed El-Kurd, José Olivarez, Noam Chomsky, Winona LaDuke, Robyn Maynard, Leanne Betasamosake Simpson, Howard Zinn, Mike Davis, Marc Lamont Hill, Dave Zirin, Astra Taylor, and Amy Goodman, among many other leading writers of our time. We are also the trade publishers of the acclaimed Historical Materialism Book Series.

Haymarket also manages a vibrant community organizing and event space in Chicago, Haymarket House, the popular Haymarket Books Live event series and podcast, and the annual Socialism Conference.

ALSO AVAILABLE FROM HAYMARKET BOOKS

Because You Were Mine
Brionne Janae

ballast
by Quenton Baker

Por Siempre
by José Olivarez and Antonio Salazar

Super Sad Black Girl
by Diamond Sharp

All the Blood Involved in Love
by Maya Marshall

DEAR GOD. DEAR BONES. DEAR YELLOW.
by Noor Hindi

The Sentences That Create Us: Crafting A Writer's Life in Prison
by PEN America, edited by Caits Meissner

I Remember Death By Its Proximity to What I Love
by Mahogany L. Browne

Doppelgangbanger
by Cortney Lamar Charleston

Mama Phife Represents: A Memoir
by Cheryl Boyce-Taylor

The Anti-Racist Writing Workshop: How To Decolonize the Creative Classroom
by Felicia Rose Chavez